4778   1009

THE TRUST FOR PUBLIC LAND
ON THE SCENE SINCE 1987

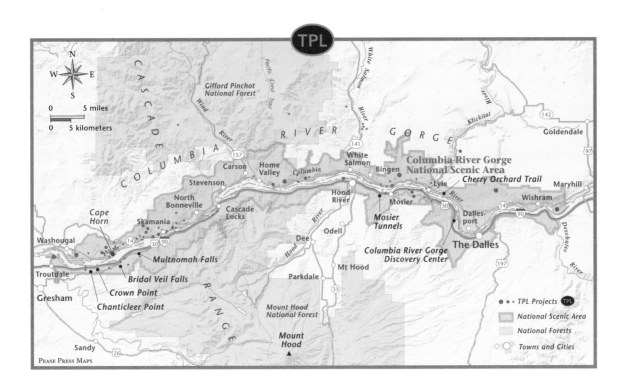

The Trust for Public Land is proud to have been at the forefront of the efforts to save the wild landscape of Columbia Gorge since 1987.

To date, we have conserved over 17,000 acres of land within the National Scenic Area—so it's hardly surprising that many of the most beautiful photographs throughout this book show landscapes that we helped to keep intact.

As you enjoy this celebration of the Columbia Gorge National Scenic Area look out for the TPL symbol next to picture captions. Each one is a sign of the efforts that have gone into preserving this natural, cultural, historic—and recreational—wonder for everyone to enjoy now, and into the future.

THE
TRUST
for
PUBLIC
LAND

TO FIND OUT MORE ABOUT THE TRUST FOR PUBLIC LAND VISIT
WWW.TPL.ORG

Peter, Janet and Beautiful America Publishing want to thank the sponsors listed below, for their support and assistance in making this book possible. Our thanks to all. Enjoy.

—————————————— ✦ ——————————————

THE TRUST FOR PUBLIC LAND (TITLE SPONSOR)

SKAMANIA LODGE

BEST WESTERN HOOD RIVER INN

INSITU, INCORPORATED

COLUMBIA RIVER GORGE VISITORS ASSOCIATION

SKAMANIA COUNTY CHAMBER OF COMMERCE

FRIENDS OF THE COLUMBIA GORGE

USDA FOREST SERVICE

PROVIDENCE HOOD RIVER MEMORIAL HOSPITAL

MULTNOMAH FALLS LODGE

WAUCOMA BOOKSTORE

COLUMBIA RIVER GORGE

NATIONAL SCENIC AREA

Camas in bloom above the Gorge, near Carson, Washington

Cover photograph: A beautiful Gorge sunset from Mitchell Point TPL

To the memory of my mother, Ethel Pochocki, whose courage, wit, and
uncompromising devotion to truth and beauty endures
— Peter Marbach

*Please note- Where you see the TPL button — The Trust for Public Land
helped conserve the land in the picture

Published by
Beautiful America Publishing Company
P.O. Box 244
Woodburn, OR 97071
www.beautifulamericapub.com

Library of Congress Catalog Number 2011010878

ISBN 978-0-89802-877-5 (hardcover)

OFFICES OF THE GOVERNORS

JOHN KITZHABER
OREGON

CHRISTINE O. GREGOIRE
WASHINGTON

In 1986, the Columbia River Gorge National Scenic Area Act created landmark legislation to protect the scenic landscapes, natural habitat, cultural resources, and outdoor recreation, while at the same time support the economic development of Gorge communities. This year, the Columbia River Gorge National Scenic Area celebrates its 25th anniversary.

In the quarter century since, the Act has created clear successes: over 40,000 acres of land acquired for public use, the restoration of the Historic Columbia River Highway, a Management Plan that has helped limit the impacts of new development, and $11 million in grants and loans to businesses in the Columbia River Gorge.

The Columbia River Gorge is like no place on earth. Volcanic eruptions and Ice Age floods have created a spectacular river canyon slicing through the Cascades Mountains. It is also home to the largest collection of waterfalls in North America and a host to wildflowers that exist nowhere else on earth.

This wild and beautiful place is more than just scenery. Rich in tribal history, it has served as a human corridor for tens of thousands of years, was explored by Lewis and Clark, and traversed by thousands of Oregon Trail pioneers. Today, the Gorge is home to over 70,000 people in 13 communities. It is a place where people make their homes, work and play every day.

The Columbia River Gorge is an international treasure. We must build upon the efforts of the first 25 years and work to inspire pride, passion, and creative thinking for the future stewardship of this special place.

John Kitzhaber
Governor of Oregon

Christine O. Gregoire
Governor of Washington

DEDICATION

We dedicate this book to a very courageous lady and a dear friend, Nancy Russell, who left us in 2008. Her love of the Gorge, and her continuing efforts to make sure it was pre-served, are legendary. Without her there would be no book, nor Gorge celebration.

—Beautiful America Publishing

COLUMBIA RIVER GORGE
NATIONAL SCENIC AREA

PHOTOGRAPHY BY PETER MARBACH

TEXT BY JANET COOK

Beautiful America Publishing Company
T.M.

The ever-shifting sand dunes of eastern Oregon

Beautiful Franz Lake National Wildlife Refuge

Happy 25th Anniversary

We think it is worthwhile to note that this wonderful year of 2011, is not only the 25th Anniversary Celebration of the COLUMBIA RIVER GORGE — National Scenic Area, but also the 25th Anniversary of BEAUTIFUL AMERICA PUBLISHING COMPANY. This very fact had been a huge deciding factor for us, when Peter came to us with his proposal. What an absolutely perfect fit!

Our very first comment to Peter was, "You know that 25 years ago, a delightful lady named, Nancy Russell called us and asked, "Would we consider doing a Columbia River Gorge Calendar? I think it would be a huge help to us and our cause in the Gorge." Our answer was an immediate "Why sure! It's the most beautiful area in the world, isn't it?" She was thrilled. We were close "Friends" ever since. And the calendar? We have done one every year for those 25 years — and it has become a very popular seller.

So as we pause to celebrate this Natural Wonder here in our backyard, we like to feel that the Columbia River Gorge Calendar had a lot to do with the National Scenic Area bill. They were that constant, visual reminder of how absolutely beautiful the Gorge really is. The Calendar, a group of people called "Friends," and a determined lady named Nancy. What a formidable group we made.

HAPPY 25th ANNIVERSARY!!

Beautiful America Publishing Company

Beverly and Ted Paul

TABLE OF CONTENTS

Spring in the Gorge from Skamania Point, Washington TPL

INTRODUCTION

It is breathtaking, this 85-mile corridor where the Columbia River carves its way through the Cascade Mountains. Eighty-five miles, beginning where the Deschutes River pours into it and ending where the river flows suddenly out of the primordial landscape of the Columbia River Gorge – whose vertical basalt walls rise 3,000 feet in places, the work of the river's incessant flow over thousands of years – and into the urban sprawl of Portland and Vancouver.

The Columbia River Gorge is one of the most ecologically diverse places on earth, supporting five major ecosystems in less than 100 miles. In the high desert microclimate of its eastern end, with annual rainfall of less than 15 inches, rocky bluffs, rolling grassy hills, ranchland and sloping vineyards define the landscape. At the western end, annual rainfall of more than 75 inches creates lush rainforests and a spectacular number of waterfalls cascading down sheer basalt cliffs. In between are arid savannas, pine-oak woodlands and pockets of marshy wetlands. The Columbia Gorge boasts more than 800 species of native wildflowers and flowering shrubs; 15 wildflowers are endemic, existing only here, in the Gorge.

The Columbia River Gorge is a place of unrivaled, wild beauty – all the more so given its close proximity to two of the Northwest's largest cities. It was precisely this proximity, and the growing urban sprawl and spotty land-use laws of the 1970s, that spurred a movement to preserve this magnificent place. The vision of strip malls, gas stations, trophy homes and subdivisions rising amid the dramatic landscapes that define the Gorge was a rallying cry to many that something must be done to preserve the Columbia River Gorge for the generations to come.

This year, we celebrate 25 years since the Columbia River Gorge National Scenic Area Act became law, in November

1986, creating an unprecedented model of land preservation. Simply, the Scenic Area Act encourages growth and economic development within the urban areas of the Gorge in order to preserve the landscapes outside of them. But it's far from simple. No other federally protected area in the country has such a complex array of stakeholders, such widely varied geography and landscapes, such a rich indigenous history that includes one of the oldest settlements in North America, nor such an improbable mandate of nurturing economic vitality while simultaneously shepherding the most rigorous of land protections. As we mark a quarter century of this evolving story, it's worth looking at the past, present and future of the Scenic Area – not only for the unique tale it is, but to see what this historic Act means to the people who live here as well as the two million people who visit the Columbia River Gorge from all over the country and around the world every year.

Lyle Point TPL

Barge passes below Friends of the Gorge Land Trust Protected Area on plateau near Celilo TPL

16

Vineyard near Mosier

Petroglyph, Tsagaglalal, "She Who Watches"

In the beginning . . .

The story of the Columbia River Gorge is, at its core, a tale of geologic events that occurred over the course of millions of years. Between 40 and 20 million years ago, the prehistoric Columbia River flowed south from its origin in what is now British Columbia, over eastern Washington to northeastern Oregon, where it turned west, as it does today. But there the similarities end, for near The Dalles, the ancestral river channel turned southwest and flowed through a 25-mile-wide valley extending across the Hood River Valley and over what is now Mount Hood. At the time, there was no mountain there, no Cascade Range – no prominent peaks at all. The river flowed across these lowlands and emptied into the ocean around where Salem now sits.

Between 16 and 6 million years ago, lava boiled incessantly from vents in Idaho and eastern Washington and flowed south and west along the ancestral Columbia River channel. Known as the Columbia River basalts, these massive lava flows occurred in several phases over 10 million years, forming much of the foundation of today's Columbia River Gorge – and leaving their legacy visible throughout it. One, known as the Priest Rapids flow, sent hot lava coursing down the Columbia where, near The Dalles, it encountered a large, shallow lake where previous flows had dammed the river. When the hot lava hit the lake water, it caused masses of hot ash and mud to push miles downriver with the lava flowing closely behind. The ensuing sediments eventually filled the Columbia's channel. Today, areas of "pillow lavas" can be seen in and around The Dalles – representing where the Priest Rapids basalt flow entered the shallow lake – and Crown Point, at the Gorge's western end, marks where the lava finally cooled and came to a halt. This flow choked off the channel of the Columbia River and forced it to move north, one step in a centuries-long march that would finally end where the river flows today.

For several million years, these lava flows raged through the Columbia River channel, filling it and forcing the river to cut yet a new channel – each time slightly different than the one before. One of the last of these flows, the Pomona flow, filled only part of the river channel. But the basalt columns from it can be seen between Hood River and The Dalles; the near-vertical columns of the Pomona flow differ from the folded and slanted columns of earlier flows.

After the Columbia River basalts ceased erupting, the oceanic plate continued to push under the continental plate, uplifting the Cascade mountains. This faulting also created the anticlines and synclines visible in many places in the Gorge – especially east of Hood River. Between about 4 million and 700,000 years ago, lava erupting from dozens of volcanos altered the Columbia River's course yet again and again, finally pushing it north to its present course.

The last ice age, from about 19,000 to 13,000 years ago, created some of the most cataclysmic floods in Earth's history – floods that carved the Columbia River Gorge as we know it today. Ice from British Columbia glaciers that spread across Washington and Idaho blocked the Clark Fork River, a Columbia River tributary, forming massive Lake Missoula. The glacial lake inundated 3,000 square miles under as much as 900 feet of water. Eventually the water burst through the ice dam, sending 500 cubic miles of water flooding across eastern Washington and into the channel of the only outlet through the Cascades – the Columbia River. The floodwaters crested at over 1,000 feet east of The Dalles. Flowing at the rate of about 10 million cubic meters per second, the floodwaters filled the Columbia River Gorge to overflowing – rushing over the top of Crown Point before spreading into the Portland Basin.

Lovely Gorge view from Cape Horn, Washington TPL

Golden sunset from Cascade Locks

As glacial ice advanced and retreated over several thousand years, floods from Lake Missoula occurred as many as 90 times, scouring the eastern Gorge and sculpting the towering cliff walls of the central and western Gorge. As the powerful Columbia cut through the layers of basalt, it left dozens of tributaries to plummet down from high above its channel. Today, one of the greatest concentrations of waterfalls in the western United States is found in the Columbia Gorge.

In our collectively egocentric world, it's easy to look at the myriad geologic events that have created the Columbia River Gorge as history. But man has inhabited the Gorge for a mere wink in geologic time. Though we've tamed the river with dams and harnessed its energy for power, built cities along its banks, and artificially altered its course to suit our needs, geologic events continue to happen as they always have. In 1996 an enormous landslide triggered by winter rains flowed down from the steep walls around Dodson, famously destroying a house that still sits among the boulders. In 2006, flooding from the Hood River spread sediment into the Columbia, creating a massive delta that changed the Hood River's confluence with the Columbia and altered much of the waterfront area of the town.

FROM PREHISTORY TO THE MODERN ERA

Not long after the last of the Missoula floods raged through the Columbia Gorge, the final glacial retreat marking the end of the last ice age began. As the climate grew milder, human migration spread. Evidence of human habitation along the Columbia dates back at least 11,000 years, as the ancestors of today's tribal people with ties to the Columbia River began living here. Over time, the population of Native Americans living in the Gorge, on both sides of the river, grew. Distinct cultures formed, with differing customs and traditions. In the western Gorge, tribes of Chinook Indians lived in permanent villages, their houses built of cedar planks. To the east, Sahaptin-speaking Indians of various tribes lived in more transient tule mat lodges. To all the Indians living up and down the Columbia, the river was the center of life. The river is known as "Wimahl" to the Chinook-speaking peoples of the lower Columbia, and "N'chi-Wana" to the Sahaptin-speaking peoples of its eastern reaches; both terms mean essentially "Big River."

The river and its boundless runs of salmon united all the people living along its banks. From just west of the Deschutes River, where the Columbia roared over Celilo Falls, for nearly 50 miles to the Cascades rapids near present-day Cascade Locks, the river toiled over the remnants of ancestral lava flows and landslides, creating ideal conditions for catching salmon as they made their way upriver to spawn. Celilo Falls and The Long Narrows, a section of river extending from a few miles below Celilo Falls to The Dalles, were the most prolific fishing areas along the river. Over thousands of years, Native families and tribes staked out their own fishing places here, building platforms and scaffolds extending out over the river where they scooped fish from the water with dipnets. Celilo Falls, whose roar was nearly deafening during the spring run-off, became

TPL Following Page: Winter in the Gorge

23

legendary for both its fishing and spiritual qualities. But The Long Narrows, where basalt rock formations forced the nearly 1,000-foot-wide Columbia to constrict into a 180-foot-wide channel, was perhaps the more popular and bountiful fishing area. Along this eight-mile-long stretch of churning, roiling river, the salmon stopped to rest in eddies near the shore, where Indians lined up practically elbow-to-elbow during the spring and fall runs.

Celilo Falls and The Narrows became a center of commerce, where tribes from north, east and south as well as downriver and the coast came to trade during the spring and fall Chinook runs. The permanent population of perhaps a few hundred swelled to thousands as Natives brought trade goods from afar and sought the signature product of Columbia River Indians: dried salmon. Produced after drying on scaffolds and then being pounded into a course powder, the dried salmon was pressed into baskets lined with cured salmon skin. This valuable concentrated protein could be stored for months and used when other foods were scarce.

The Celilo market also served as a great social gathering where Indians from hundreds of miles away and from many different tribes came together to feast, sing, dance, play games, gamble, find mates and participate in religious ceremonies. Artifacts dating back 11,000 years have been found near Celilo Falls, proving it to be one of the oldest continuously occupied settlements in North America. Celilo Falls was not only a sacred fishing place for hundreds of generations of Indians, it also was one of the longest-running market places in the history of man.

Due perhaps to the vagaries of geologic events like landslides and floods, fewer Indians lived downriver in the heart of the Columbia Gorge. But small bands of Natives spent at least certain seasons here, where berries proliferated and camas and wapato roots could be dug from the lush meadows fronting the river. Some time around 600 years ago, the last and largest of several major landslides occurred in the central Gorge, altering life for those living along the river here. The Bonneville Slide brought massive amounts of rock down from Table Mountain, above Stevenson, sprawling 14 square miles and sending debris across the river to form a dam. The resulting land bridge gave rise to the Indian legend of the Bridge of the Gods, and provided – at least for a time – the Natives on both sides of the river with an easy crossing. Eventually, the powerful Columbia River eroded its way through. But the slide left its mark in the form of the miles-long Cascades Rapids which became, like the Long Narrows, a rich fishing ground – as well as one of the most treacherous stretches of the Columbia River.

The first white men to arrive in the Columbia Gorge were Meriwether Lewis and William Clark and their expedition, which traveled west down the Gorge in the fall of 1805. The explorers wrote in detail of their dangerous descents through and portages around Celilo Falls and the Narrows, and farther downriver at the Cascades – a section of which Clark described: "This Great shute or falls is about 1/2 a mile, with the water of this great river compressed within the space of 150 paces in which there is great numbers of both large and small rocks, water passing with great velocity [foaming] & boiling in a most horriable manner. ..."

Lewis and Clark's expedition camped in several places in the Gorge on its way west and on its return east in the spring of 1806 – which proved to be an even more difficult journey due to the spring run-off from the snowy Cascades. Lewis remarked that "the water appears to be (considerably) upwards of 20 feet higher than when we descended the river." The famous Gorge winds also hampered their progress, often creating waves

Dynamic Basalt Arch near Biggs, Oregon

Tough shot--Cigar Rock at Cape Horn TPL

Opposite: Striking St. Peter's Dome in the Gorge

several feet high. At one point around the Cascades, it took the group three days to travel seven miles. Despite human habitation in the Gorge for 11,000 years or more, the journals are the first written record of life in the Columbia River Gorge.

Lewis and Clark's expedition led more explorers to the Gorge. As Fort Astoria and Fort Vancouver became trade centers of the Northwest, fur trappers plied the Columbia River and its tributaries. European trade goods found their way to Indians living in the Gorge, as did European diseases. Where they had prospered for millennia, rich in body and spirit from the river's bounty, Native Americans began dying by the hundreds. By the early 1800s, as much as 90 percent of the Native population had been decimated by smallpox, measles, tuberculosis and other deadly diseases brought by the white man.

In the 1830s, the first emigrants began to arrive on the nascent Oregon Trail, lured by the promise of cheap agricultural land in the Willamette Valley. Despite the hardships endured on the 2,000-mile trek across the country, by many accounts the most treacherous part of the trip was the last 75 miles down the Columbia River from The Dalles to Portland – for here, it essentially became a water route. Emigrants loaded their possessions and wagons onto log rafts or into dugout canoes. At the Cascades, they used the same primitive Indian trail Lewis and Clark had to portage several miles around the rapids. Diaries of pioneers tell harrowing tales of the journey. One emigrant wrote in 1844 that he "found men in the prime of life lying among the rocks," seemingly ready to die. The trip down the river was so dangerous that, in 1845, a nearly equally formidable toll route over the south side of Mt. Hood was built, known as the Barlow Road. Although the route was long, with sections so steep that wagons had to be painstakingly winched down, pioneers often favored this route over the river descent.

As more and more emigrants arrived on the Oregon Trail, The Dalles prospered. The Oregon Territory was established in 1848, and the military erected Fort Dalles in 1850. With the growth of the city and the strategic importance of the fort – as well as others to the east – the Columbia Gorge became a vital supply route. In order to ensure the flow of goods upriver, the military erected three forts along the Cascades in the 1850s. In 1855, pressured by government officials and increasingly encroached upon by white settlers, several Columbia River Indian tribes signed treaties with the U.S. government, creating reservations for the Umatilla, the Nez Perce, the Yakima and the Warm Springs. The tribes retained fishing and ceremonial rights on the Columbia River in perpetuity.

The 1850s ushered in a century-long era of change along the Columbia River that would forever alter life in the Gorge. Steam-driven paddleboats carrying passengers and goods began plying the Columbia – giving rise to the logging industry as industrious entrepreneurs made a living cutting wood to supply the steamboats, as well as to provide heat for the growing population of The Dalles and other Gorge towns. The Cascades, The Long Narrows and Celilo Falls were impassible barriers to contiguous river travel, forcing passengers and freight to portage between boats for miles on primitive trails. This inconvenience led to construction of the first crude railway in the Gorge, a three-mile portage rail around the Cascades that followed the ancient Indian trail on the river's north bank. By the 1880s, there were more than 20 miles of portage railroads operating in the Gorge, powered by steam locomotives.

During the second half of the 1800s, both settlers and exploiters of the Gorge sought more efficient ways to harvest its natural resources. Permanent and floating fishwheels operated

Beautiful restored interior of Vista House

Scenic favorite, Vista House, perched high atop Crown Point

up and down the river, capable of scooping up as much as 70,000 pounds of fish a day. By the 1880s, more than 40 fish canneries were in full swing along the Columbia between Astoria and the Deschutes River – including two of the largest located near the historic fisheries of the Cascades and Celilo Falls.

Native Americans had paid careful attention to maintaining fish populations for tens of thousands of years, allowing plenty of salmon to make their way past them to their spawning grounds and holding sacred ceremonies devoted to ensuring the eternity of the salmon runs. But in less than three decades of commercial fishing, the salmon industry peaked in the mid-1880s, when more than 40-million pounds of fish were caught annually. Then began a long, permanent decline.

In the late 1800s, industrialists seeking easier passage through the Columbia Gorge constructed Cascade Locks and Canal, completed in 1896. For the first time, boats could travel unhindered past the dangerous Cascades of the Columbia. The Celilo Canal, bypassing Celilo Falls, opened in 1915. But the biggest change to the river came with the completion of Bonneville Dam in 1937. As water pooled behind the dam, the dangerous Cascades rapids churned briefly just below the surface, then were gone forever. The dam brought cheap hydropower to the region but further reduced salmon populations.

Upriver from Bonneville, the Columbia retained its ancient course for 20 years more until, on the morning of March 10, 1957, the gates of The Dalles Dam shut. Within hours, the Long Narrows was drowned beneath the rising water, followed by Celilo Falls, whose ancient deafening roar would be heard no more.

THE PUSH FOR PRESERVATION

Interest in preservation of the Columbia River Gorge waxed and waned through the early and mid-20th century – beginning in 1915 with the opening of the Columbia River Highway, the nation's first scenic highway. Promoters of the road convinced benefactors to purchase waterfalls and other scenic places along the route – which eventually traversed the Gorge from Troutdale to The Dalles – to preserve as parks for tourists. Eventually, there were 21 state parks up and down the Gorge on the Oregon side.

By the 1930s, the popularity of the Columbia River Highway had brought so many visitors to the Gorge that development concerns arose. In 1937, the Pacific Northwest Regional Planning Commission declared that the Columbia Gorge was an area of national significance and proposed establishing it as an interstate park. World War II interrupted the growing interest in protecting the resources of the Gorge, but in the 1950s the focus returned and both Oregon and Washington created gorge commissions. They had limited effect, however, due to inadequate funding, lack of authority and opposition from various factions.

In the 1970s, concern for the fate of the Columbia River Gorge heightened with the proposal for the I-205 bridge linking east Portland and Vancouver. Long before the bridge was completed in 1982, miles of country lanes and farmland on both sides of the Columbia River had been turned into subdivisions that threatened to spread ever farther east, into the Gorge. Plans for industrial developments at the mouth of the Gorge were also in the works. At about the same time, the U.S. Park Service released a report indicating an increase in development pressures in the Gorge. As if on cue, Skamania County approved a 24-lot subdivision on a prominent hillside across from

Beacon Rock in Beacon Rock State Park

Opposite: Beautiful major attraction, Multnomah Falls

Multnomah Falls. Realizing that protection would have to come from the federal government, alarmed preservationists and Gorge-lovers turned to Oregon Senator Mark Hatfield for help. Hatfield agreed he would support and push for federal legislation as long as he had a broad coalition – from both sides of the river and the political aisle – standing behind him.

To build that coalition, Portland conservationist and long-time advocate of Gorge protection John Yeon (a well-known architect whose father had been construction manager of the Columbia River Highway) enlisted the help of an unlikely hero: a Portland housewife named Nancy Russell.

Along with being a busy mother of four children, Russell was a lover of wildflowers. She raised plants from seed in her hillside garden and organized a conservation program with the Portland Garden Club. When her youngest child became school-aged, she often would see her kids onto the school bus, then drive out to the Gorge to spend the day hiking amid the hundreds of species of wildflowers that flourish up and down the river. She knew the Gorge like the back of her hand and loved it fiercely.

She agreed to lead the fight for federal protection of the Columbia Gorge and, in 1980, co-founded Friends of the Columbia Gorge to push for federal protection. She recruited a high-powered board of directors hailing from both Oregon and Washington, including ex-Oregon governors Tom McCall and Bob Straub, ex-Washington governor Dan Evans (who would become a U.S. senator in 1983, providing critical support for the Scenic Area Act in Congress), and Portland city commissioner Mike Lindberg.

The fact that she had little experience with non-profits and none with fundraising or lobbying mattered little once Russell set her sights on protecting the Gorge. Beneath her friendly demeanor was a fierce competitiveness and resolve; she simply didn't give up. Fortunately, she also had thick skin, which she would need over the next six years as she became the face of the controversial issue of federal protection of the Columbia Gorge.

The Friends of the Columbia Gorge spent most of its time working to develop federal legislation to protect the Gorge; attorney Bowen Blair, who served as Friends' executive director from 1982-88, wrote much of the legislation, shuttling between Washington, D.C., and the Oregon and Washington statehouses negotiating terms with lawmakers. Russell often accompanied him, and worked tirelessly to build public support for federal protection. Friends of the Gorge also challenged what they considered inappropriate development proposals, including the plan for a subdivision across from Multnomah Falls and another near Beacon Rock. Both were halted through lawsuits initiated by Friends. As these fights drew out, it became only more obvious to supporters of Gorge protection that, without a single public entity to exercise authority over land-use decisions, the Gorge would become a land grab.

Not everyone felt the same, however. The logging companies that owned or managed large swaths of land in Skamania and Klickitat counties formed a strong and well-funded opposition. Residents of these and other affected counties – many of whom were descended from the Gorge's first loggers – resented the idea of federal intervention in local land-use issues. Still others disliked the idea of an "outsider" – a Portlander – meddling in their affairs. Some were simply fierce private property rights advocates. One vociferous opposition group, Columbia Gorge United, distributed bumper stickers that read, "Save the Gorge from Nancy Russell."

Evening at Rooster Rock State Park

Autumn at Shepperd's Dell Falls

Even within the drive to create federal protection, there were disagreements of how best to go about it. One vocal faction advocated turning the Gorge into a national park. With adherents from the myriad camps attending in droves, all nine of the major state and federal hearings held from 1981 to 1986 on the fate of the Columbia Gorge were notoriously acrimonious. But Russell never backed down. Along with the bumper stickers, she endured numerous personal threats. After one all-day hearing in Skamania County, she found her tires slashed. Another time, she opened her front door to find a detractor threatening her. Before her death in 2008, Russell told an interviewer that she didn't mind taking the heat as long as she was protecting the people who could get things done.

A series of proposed bills failed in Congress over the course of several years. Finally in the fall of 1986, with some favorable changes in the Washington Congressional delegation and governorship, as well as Oregon's strength in both the House and Senate, the Columbia River Gorge National Scenic Area Act passed – just hours before it would have died from a pocket veto. There was both celebration among supporters of the legislation and anger among detractors. According to Senator Hatfield, who was present at the occasion, President Ronald Reagan held his nose as he signed the Act on November 17, 1986. The flags at the Skamania County government building flew at half-staff.

The first 25 years

The Columbia River Gorge National Scenic Area Act created the first, and still the only, legislated Scenic Area in the country that encompassed both public and private land and which included cities and towns within its borders. It designated for federal protection 292,500 acres on both sides of the Columbia River, from the Sandy River to the Deschutes River in Oregon, and from Gibbons Creek in Clark County, Wash., to a line four miles east of Wishram. The Scenic Area includes parts of six counties: Multnomah, Hood River and Wasco counties in Oregon; and Clark, Skamania and Klickitat counties in Washington. Within the Scenic Area there are 13 cities and towns designated as Urban Areas in the Act: Cascade Locks, Hood River, Mosier and The Dalles in Oregon; and North Bonneville, Stevenson, Carson, Home Valley, White Salmon, Bingen, Lyle, Dallesport and Wishram in Washington.

The crux of the Scenic Area Act lies in its two interwoven purposes: 1) To establish a national scenic area to protect and provide for the enhancement of the scenic, cultural, recreational, and natural resources of the Columbia River Gorge; and 2) To protect and support the economy of the Columbia River Gorge area by encouraging growth to occur in existing urban areas and by allowing future economic development in a manner that is consistent with purpose 1. The Scenic Area Act, in other words, strives to achieve an unprecedented balance between preservation and development.

The 292,500 acres that comprise the Scenic Area are divided into three categories: 115,100 acres of Special Management Areas (SMA), primarily the region's most sensitive lands where little development is allowed; 149,400 acres of General Management Areas (GMA), which include areas with a mixture of historic land uses such as agriculture and logging; and about 28,500 acres of

Mt. Hood looms over the Columbia Gorge Hotel and Columbia Cliff Villas

Beautiful Columbia Gorge Hotel

Urban Areas. Another unique aspect of the Scenic Area is its governance: responsibility for managing the Scenic Area falls on several partners, including the USDA Forest Service, four Native American tribes, the six counties and 13 cities in the Scenic Area, and a bi-state entity called the Columbia River Gorge Commission.

The Gorge Commission, an entity created by the legislation, is funded in equal amounts by Oregon and Washington. The commission is comprised of 13 members: three appointed by each of the governors of Oregon and Washington, one appointed by each of the six Gorge counties, and one (nonvoting) representative from the Forest Service. The Gorge Commission oversees land use and development in the GMA, while the Forest Service manages the SMA. The Urban Areas are exempt from the Scenic Area legislation. A Management Plan – developed over the course of four years by the Gorge Commission and the Forest Service, with input from tribal governments, county and city governments, state and federal organizations and citizens – details development and preservation guidelines and helps the Gorge Commission rule on land-use disputes and other controversies within the Scenic Area.

With passage of the Scenic Area Act came some deal-sweeteners in the form of federal money for economic development projects, contingent upon counties adopting land-use ordinances implementing the Scenic Area Management Plan. There would be $5 million for an interpretive center in one of the Washington counties and $5 million for a conference center in one of the Oregon counties. There was also $2.8 million set aside for restoration of the Historic Columbia River Highway, $10 million for recreation facilities and another $10 million to be available for economic development grants.

In the first years following passage of the Columbia River Gorge National Scenic Area Act, divisiveness remained between supporters and detractors of the legislation. Skamania and Klickitat counties filed lawsuits claiming the Scenic Area Act was illegal. Many of the public hearings held during creation of the Management Plan resembled in hostility those in the six years leading to passage of the Act. The Scenic Act was being implemented at the same time controversies over endangered fish and wildlife – in particular the Northern Spotted Owl – were playing out on the national stage. Logging, a mainstay in many of the counties affected by the Scenic Area Act, became increasingly restricted. Mills were crippled or shuttered entirely and unemployment was high. For some, the federal Scenic Area Act provided a scapegoat.

With time, opposition to the legislation decreased, easing still more with the adoption of the Scenic Area Management Plan in 1991. With the downturn in logging, economic development funds authorized by the Act became more enticing. After competing with Clark and Klickitat counties, Skamania County won the $5 million in federal funding for creation of a conference center. The county – once almost uniformly against the Scenic Area Act – worked diligently to create a partnership that would use the federal money in combination with other public and private investments. Just two years after adoption of the Management Plan, Skamania Lodge opened in 1993 a few miles west of Stevenson, the county seat where flags flew at half-staff after passage of the Scenic Area Act seven years before. The four-story Cascadian-style lodge, constructed with native stone and century-old timbers, has become a regionally and nationally renowned destination, as well as a popular conference center and wedding venue. Located near where the Cascades of the Columbia once roared over a long-ago landslide, Skamania Lodge is named in honor of the Chinook Indian word for "swift water."

Fall color on the Historic Gorge Highway

Opposite: Beautiful Oneonta Falls in the Oneonta Gorge

49

Likewise, Wasco County earned the $5 million for an interpretive center, and the Columbia Gorge Discovery Center opened on a bend in the river west of The Dalles in 1997 – not far from where Lewis and Clark camped for several days in 1805. Exhibits highlight the cataclysmic geologic history of the Gorge, its unique flora and fauna as well as 11,000 years of cultural history. The Discovery Center's appealing design and quality exhibits have made it a cultural center of the Gorge.

Even as the legislated changes began taking place in the Columbia Gorge, another force was at work which would prove symbiotic with the two purposes of the Scenic Area Act: the wind. In the late 1970s – about the time Nancy Russell and others began their drive for federal protection – a handful of windsurfers had discovered the Columbia Gorge and its steady west wind, which had been blowing from spring to fall through the funnel-like Gorge since time immemorial. Word spread, and by the mid-1980s the Columbia Gorge, with Hood River as its epicenter, was gaining national prominence as a windsurfing destination. To these newcomers the Scenic Area Act, with one of its main premises being to enhance recreational resources, was just one more reason to love the Gorge.

The attraction of windsurfers to the Gorge led to its outing in ever-widening circles as a recreation mecca in general. There were miles of river with world-class whitewater for kayakers. Ditto mountain biking trails, hiking trails, and winding rural roads for roadbiking. Skiing and snowboarding – even in the summer on the Palmer Glacier at Timberline Resort – were less than an hour's drive from shore of the Columbia River. The federal protection of so much acreage opened up even more land to the public, much of it well maintained by Forest Service staff and volunteers.

And so the Scenic Area Act, in both subtle and overt ways, launched a reshaping of the Gorge economy. The Historic Columbia River Highway – the road that first brought droves of tourists to the Gorge nearly a century ago – became a draw once again. The Act called for restoration of ramshackle portions of the road that had been inaccessible for decades. This included much of the old highway through the heart of the Gorge from Warrendale to Mosier. After passage of the Scenic Area Act, the Oregon legislature directed the Oregon Department of Transportation to plan for restoring and reconnecting the scenic route as a State Trail. Over the last 25 years, all but a few miles of the Historic Columbia River Highway have been returned to their original splendor – now as a hiking and biking trail. The highway is listed on the National Register of Historic Places and is a National Historic Landmark.

Many area fruit growers took advantage of the rise in tourism by retooling their businesses. Historically agricultural lands were protected under the Scenic Area Act, and many local fruit growers opened their orchards and farms for tours and U-pick fruit selling, and established on-site farm stands. The Hood River County Fruit Loop was organized in 1992 as a way to showcase the Hood River Valley's array of fruit growers and family farms. The 35-mile scenic loop features more than 30 farms and has become a regional and national destination.

As agri-tourism was on the rise, a few orchardists also began to diversify their plantings by adding wine grapes. The dramatic geophysical differences present along the Columbia Gorge – with a wetter, cooler climate in the west changing to hotter, drier conditions in the east, as well as varied elevations and proximities to the thermal mass of the Columbia River – translated into a jackpot of microclimates ideal for growing a

Low tide reveals ancient boulders at Cigar Rock TPL

Kolk pond formed during ice age floods TPL

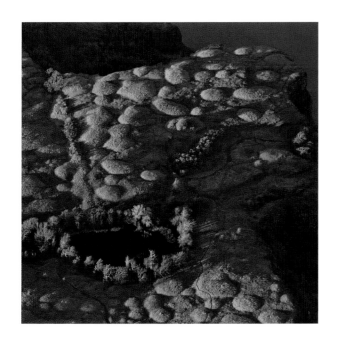

Biscuit Scablands at Rowena Plateau TPL

Ancient Basalt Arch near Catherine Creek TPL

wide variety of grapes. Some areas previously thought of as low-value farmland proved ideal for viticulture. The reputation for quality wines from the Columbia River Gorge spread and, in 2004, a 191,000-acre area straddling the river in the central Gorge received federal designation as an official American Viticulture Area – the Columbia Gorge AVA.

The region has continued to grow as a player in the wine industry. Its rich and varied soils accumulated from floods, volcanic eruptions and landslides grow more than 30 varieties of grapes on more than 50 vineyards. The Columbia Gorge AVA markets itself as "a world of wine in 40 miles," with more than 30 wineries catering to the growing wine tourism market. The many vineyards visible up and down the river are one of the few changes in the landscape of the Gorge over the last quarter century, as most of them didn't exist when the Scenic Area Act was passed.

The emphasis on agriculture in the Gorge also led to the creation of the Gorge Grown Food Network, a nonprofit launched in 2006 as a way to connect local farmers with local consumers. What started with a handful of local growers has grown exponentially; there are now more than 80 farmer members of Gorge Grown, from Stevenson to Biggs. Many are so-called community-supported agriculture, or CSA, farms, where members pay annually for weekly food deliveries from the farm. A mainstay of the organization is a weekly farmer's market held in Hood River as a means to get fresh, local food to consumers and give farmers a profitable means of selling their goods. Thanks in part to Gorge Grown, many area restaurants also base their menus on what's available locally and seasonally.

As historic economic mainstays like logging and heavy industry dwindled, other businesses filled the vacuum. Dozens of windsurfing companies and other outdoor recreation firms were launched in the Gorge, or moved headquarters here from somewhere else. A small army of entrepreneurs have begun all manner of businesses in the Gorge – many of them started by one-time visitors to the area who decided to stay for the lifestyle it offered. A notable rise in high-tech firms in the Gorge has also taken place over the past decade – some homegrown and others connected to global players; Google has an extensive data center campus on the waterfront in The Dalles, located near where there was once an aluminum smelter. Businesses catering to sustainable products also proliferate, and Columbia Gorge Community College, based in The Dalles, offers one of the country's foremost renewable energy technology training programs. Nearly all these changes evolved as part of the Scenic Area legislation's goal to shift economic activity to the urban areas of the Gorge.

While the Columbia Gorge landed on the national and international map for its wide array of tourism draws, other things have played out in the Scenic Area less visibly – but no less significantly – over the last 25 years. The Scenic Area legislation directed the Forest Service to work to acquire private lands that were patchworked within the Scenic Area. For several years after passage of the Act, landowners could receive pre-Scenic Area appraisals for their land, and many sold their parcels rather than be subject to the restrictive guidelines for development within the Scenic Area. Land trusts – The Trust for Public Land, in particular and, more recently, Friends of the Columbia Gorge Land Trust – have played a significant role in this realm.

Spring at Major Creek in Washington TPL

Wildflowers along Coyote Wall Trail in eastern Gorge TPL

The Trust for Public Land – one of whose board members was Nancy Russell – began buying significant properties and holding them during the early 1980s as a way to demonstrate that the push for Gorge protection was real and viable. Since passage of the Scenic Area Act, TPL has continued to purchase properties from willing sellers and hold them until the Forest Service can obtain federal appropriations to buy them for folding in to the public lands of the Scenic Area. More than 80 properties have been acquired in this manner, many of them beloved places in the Gorge whose names alone evoke emotion: Steigerwald Lake, Cape Horn, the Pillars of Hercules, Beacon Rock, Dog Mountain, Coyote Wall, Memaloose Hills, Dalles Mountain Ranch, Miller Island.

Other much-loved places are part of the Scenic Area thanks to Nancy Russell, who – with the support of her husband, Bruce – was a sort of Gorge land trust unto herself for nearly 30 years. She worked closely with TPL – sometimes providing funds for their land purchases – but also bought more than 30 parcels of land herself totaling over 600 acres, many of which she sold to the Forest Service at well below market value, and others which she merely opened up for public access. She was instrumental in preserving Cape Horn, a breathtaking vista off Washington Highway 14 at the west end of the Gorge, extending a no-interest loan to TPL to purchase the remaining lots in a subdivision begun there before passage of the Scenic Area Act. A single house built in the subdivision was eventually bought by Friends of the Columbia Gorge and disassembled. A few years before her death, Russell sold another parcel of land at Cape Horn to Skamania County – at less than half its value –

to help complete the Cape Horn Trail. Russell left her mark even on the Historic Columbia River Highway; when restoration of the Twin Tunnels section of the highway was suspended due to funding problems, the Russells donated $500,000 to see the project through.

Rock of Ages Arch near Ainsworth

Summer at Horsethief Butte State Park

THE FUTURE

The Columbia River Gorge National Scenic Area, after a quarter century, has evolved as a model of land protection and economic vitality. These two often disparate goals co-exist here like no place else in the country – or maybe even the world. In a notable affirmation of the legacy of the last 25 years, National Geographic Society's Center for Sustainable Destinations in 2009 ranked the Columbia River Gorge the sixth most sustainable destination in the world – second in the nation – based on the scoring of hundreds of judges in categories of environmental quality, social and cultural integrity, historic buildings and archaeological sites, aesthetic appeal, tourism management and outlook for the future. One of the primary reasons for its high ranking, according to the judges, was that the region "benefits from some of the best land-preservation programs in the nation."

But the Columbia River Gorge faces many challenges in the next 25 years, and beyond. Increasing numbers of tourists and residents, as well as agricultural needs, will vie for decreasing amounts of water as aquifers in some Gorge towns continue to recede. Climate change could further affect water issues, as well as have other impacts on the Gorge. Urban growth boundaries in some communities will need to be adjusted to accommodate growth. Renewable energy issues loom, from evolving regulations regarding residential solar panels and wind turbines to the siting of large-scale wind turbine projects within the viewshed of the Scenic Area. Development pressures continue to be felt, with current proposals for a tribal casino and a large destination resort on the site of a former mill promising controversial decisions. Continuing to foster economic growth while protecting the resources of the Gorge – especially in a more tenuous economy – will be a significant challenge in the years ahead. Funding for the Gorge Commission itself has diminished with the recent state budget crisis, forcing the very regulatory body charged with addressing these and a myriad of other issues to confront increasing challenges with fewer resources.

But the legacy of the Columbia River Gorge National Scenic Area, at a quarter century, is etched into the landscape as surely as the Missoula floods and the soul of the Columbia River Indian people. It's the legacy of the mutual sustenance of cities and towns and the wild places in between. It's the legacy of hard work and collaboration among many to preserve a beloved place. We are all part of the legacy, the 70,000 people who live in the Gorge and the more than two million people who visit each year. And we are all responsible for how it gets passed on to the next generations – for the story of the Columbia River Gorge that our children's children will know, and live, and pass on to their children.

Winter's mantle at Metlako Falls

A Bald Eagle at Balfour Park in the Gorge TPL

Spring wildflowers at the Tom McCall Nature Preserve

Autumn at lovely Horsetail Falls

Tundra Swans on Mirror Lake

Stately Heron at Eagle Creek TPL

Hay bales near Steigerwall National Wildlife Refuge, Washington TPL

Tight turns, Historic Gorge Highway at Rowena Point

Following page: Beautiful moonrise in the Gorge below Cape Horn TPL

71

Sternwheeler Columbia Gorge

Beautiful Bridge of the Gods

Overlook at Mark O. Hatfield State Park

Fish counter at Bonneville Dam

Golf at Skamania Lodge overlooking the Gorge

Friends of the Gorge hiking on Silver Star Mountain

Windsurfing in the Gorge

Sailboat racing in the Gorge

Essays for Columbia River Gorge 25th Anniversary Commemorative Edition

JILL ARENS

The passage of the National Scenic Area Act in 1986 positioned Gorge communities to attain an ideal unlike any other region in the country — to protect this magnificent place and support a vital, robust economy. Neither goal would jeopardize the other. The Gorge Commission has worked within this guiding legislation to reach across county lines, fence lines and reservation boundaries to manage the bottom line: safeguarding the irreplaceable Columbia Gorge. At the 25-year mark, we can see the results of hammering out collaborative decisions, thinking regionally and reaching for sustainable outcomes: the Gorge continues to be a treasure grounded in the deep, rich relationships that bind us to one another.

The profound beauty of the Gorge, however, does not shield it from the complex issues. The struggles may be even more intense in the Gorge because there is so much at stake. The work of the Gorge Commission is to balance the push and pull of a sustainable life — taking care of the earth, earning a living and providing a healthy place for people to live. Indian people, who have lived here for thousands of years, work diligently to protect their treaty rights. More than two million people travel to the Gorge each year to hike, windsurf, kiteboard, fish and bike. The Gorge is a major transportation corridor for barges, railroads and highway traffic. Salmon navigate a complex river system that delivers regional hydropower, provides transportation between the interior West and the Pacific Ocean, and supports a commercial and tribal fishery.

The complementary and conflicting perspectives found here are both the weakness and strength of the Gorge. There will never be agreement on how the Scenic Area should be managed. But conflicting opinions also offer a fertile opportunity to make decisions grounded in diversity, representative of many voices and perspectives. The Gorge Commission is exceedingly fortunate to fulfill the charge that brings together so many communities to transcend politics, ideology, county, state and tribal boundaries. The Scenic Act was groundbreaking for its time, and today, looking back at 25 years of management and collaboration, it remains principled and visionary legislation. We are fortunate to have this guide to take us forward into the next 25 years, ensuring that the Columbia River Gorge retains its beauty and power, continuing to be, I am sure of this, the most exquisite place on earth.

Arens is executive director of the Columbia River Gorge Commission

Beautiful Stonehenge

Maryhill Museum

View of the Dalles, from Kelly Park

ANTONE MINTHORNE

Since time immemorial the Chinook, Wyam, Wishram, Akaitchis, Atanumlema, Chimnapum, Deschutes, Klinquit, Kowasayee, John Day, Liaywas, Ochechote, Pisko, Pishquitpah, Shyik, Skinpah, Sokulk, Tilkuni, Tushepaw, Wahowpun, Klickitat, Nez Perce, Palouse, Tenino, Tygh, Umatilla, Walla Walla and Yakama Indians lived along the N'Chi Wana (Big River), now called the Columbia River. These People, my People, possess a deep and abiding respect for the river. Its waters give life to our bodies, life to our foods, life to our communities, and life to our economy. We have always protected the abundant resources the river provides in the gorge; salmon, roots, berries, and water. Our cultures held a common belief that we were to be the "wakanish naknowee thluma" (keeper's of the salmon) and therefore we held a covenant with the salmon and the waters they swam in to steward these resources, as a gift from Creator.

When Lewis and Clark came upon the Big River, they lacked the knowledge of how big and strong the river would be, nor did they know that the region was home to dozens of tribes and Native peoples who had been the stewards since time immemorial. President Jefferson had given them the following order: "The object of your mission, is to explore the Missouri river, and such principal stream of it, as, by its course and communication with the waters of the Pacific Ocean, whether the Columbia, Oregan, Colorado or any other river may offer the most direct & practicable water communication across this continent for the purposes of commerce." The primary focus for exploration of this region was for commerce, not just for discovery. Therefore, we, as Native people mark the 25th anniversary of the Columbia River Gorge Scenic Area Act with recognition that our non-Indian friends also revere this landscape, just as we have since time began. The Act strives to maintain a balance between environmental, political, social, cultural and economic interests. The act recognizes the need for all of our common interests in protecting and preserving this magnificent landscape that is now called the Columbia River Gorge so we can stand united in stewarding this magnificent resource and scenic wonder.

Minthorne, a member of the Confederated Tribes of the Umatilla Indian Reservation, is a Columbia River Gorge Commissioner

Canoes arrive for 50-year remembrance of silencing of Celilo Falls

Pow wow at Celilo Village Longhouse

ELLEN MORRIS BISHOP

To a geologist, the Columbia River Gorge is passage, conduit, and connection. The Gorge and its potent river bind together Northwest's latte-laden west side with the open landscapes of the east. Without the river and its gorge, Oregon's coastline would be a flat expanse of sandy beaches, with few headlands to punctuate the shore. Without its passage for floodwaters, Willamette Valley soils would be less fertile, and its vineyards less distinctive. Without this conduit for winds and energy, the west side would be a darker place, and lattes harder to come by.

The Columbia River did not always flow exactly here. Some 20 million years ago the river sashayed through an ancestral gorge, about where Mount Hood rises now. This long-vanished valley provided a passage for the river—and also lavas that erupted 16 to 12 million years ago in eastern Washington and Oregon. Many of these lavas flowed through the ancient Columbia's gorge. Some reached the Pacific where they form Yaquina Head, Haystack Rock, and most of Oregon's rugged coastal scenery. As lavas repeatedly filled the old gorge, the river doggedly shifted its course northward, carving a new channel every time it was blocked by lava. Today, the Columbia River Gorge's somber sides reveal the great lava flows that bear its name—the Columbia River basalts. The gorge connects us with them as no other place.

There are other connections. The Gorge served as a conduit for raging Ice Age floods that stripped soils from eastern Washington and graciously deposited them in the Willamette Valley. Salmon and lampreys join desert and ocean in their passage through the Gorge. Eastside winds and waters course through the Gorge's narrow confines, powering westside cities. The Columbia River Gorge's elegant landscapes remind us that, eastside and westside, we are not alone, we are connected, and that despite our differences, we are one.

Bishop is a geologist, teacher and author of *In Search of Ancient Oregon: A Geological and Natural History*

Columbia Gorge Discovery Center

Lewis & Clark Wildlife Records at the Maya Lin, Bird Blind, Confluence Project, Sandy River Delta TPL

Justin Bauer, Forest Service staff teaches stream ecology to elementary students

Ryan Ojerio instructs WTA Trail Maintenance TPL

DAN HARKENRIDER

People have had a strong connection to the Columbia River Gorge for over 10,000 years. Given this long human connection to the Gorge it is only natural that conflict and turmoil would arise regarding its management and protection. Not surprisingly, this same conflict gave rise to a shared appreciation for the need to protect the natural resources and human livelihoods associated with the Columbia River Gorge.

The Columbia River Gorge is a natural resource-rich and human-enriched environment; an environment that demands our attention and respect, and for the last 25 years the Columbia River Gorge National Scenic Area has received that special attention. As I write this I am completing my tenth year as Area Manager for the National Scenic Area of the Forest Service. These last 10 years have not been without controversy or conflict, yet I am fortunate to be able to live and work in an environment where people care about the natural resource decisions being made. People living in the Gorge and in the nearby metropolitan areas have been involved in the work associated with protecting and enhancing the resources of the National Scenic Area. Diverse interests have come together to craft workable and responsible management plans for activities such as hiking, biking, horseback riding, dog walking, rail-to-trail developments, dam removal, and many other recreation and restoration projects. Working with competing interests in order to find common ground can be frustrating, is always a challenge, and is often very satisfying.

As I look to the future, I think that our efforts to protect and enhance this special place will always be a challenge given the nature of human demands on the environment. I believe our collective responsibility requires that we continue to invest time, talent, and treasure in the places we care about to ensure future generations will be able to experience and enjoy them. This may seem a tall order, but I am optimistic because in my years here I have witnessed that level of commitment from diverse interests time and time again. I hope that future generations will be grateful for the work and sacrifice that we have collectively made today to protect this place we call the Columbia River Gorge.

Harkenrider is Area Manager for the USDA Forest Service in the Columbia River Gorge National Scenic Area

Vineyard at Maryhill Winery in Washington

Wine tasting at Cathedral Ridge Winery

GERRY FRANK

  I spent many a summer day at the country home of my great-uncle, Julius Meier, dubbed Menucha, a Jewish term meaning "rest"; thus Menucha was a restful place, especially for Uncle Julius. He could be at this grand spot overlooking the Columbia River, away from the hustle bustle of his Meier & Frank retail duties and later, those of the governance of this state as our governor from 1931 to 1935. (He did not seek a second term).

  At a very young age I was aware that this was a special place with extraordinary beauty; yet, I, like many others, took the Gorge grandeur for granted, perhaps even our due as Oregonians. I came to appreciate the importance of legally protecting it from the encroachment of a growing state and country mostly through the indefatigable efforts of the late Nancy Russell, the wife of one of my dearest friends, Bruce

Russell, also now deceased. Nancy sat as chair of the Friends of the Columbia Gorge and took her responsibility seriously, giving tirelessly and generously of her time and the Russell resources. She's been deservedly honored for her foresight and leadership. My awareness of this great place within Oregon's borders was spiked by Nancy's many visits to the D.C. office of Senator Mark Hatfield for whom I served as chief-of-staff. Senator Hatfield agreed wholeheartedly with Nancy's efforts and worked hard on behalf of the Friends of the Gorge; however, in my 26 years with the Senator, Nancy's dogged lobbying topped all others. Mark finally said to me, "She's a friend of yours; you talk to her!"

Thanks should go to Senator Mark Hatfield in getting this important legislation through Congress. But it is safe to say that without Nancy Russell, the Columbia Gorge would not be protected as it is today. She leaves an admirable legacy, the epitome of what one person can do with organization and determination. I am proud to have played a small part as a conduit and supporter of both of my friends and colleagues, Nancy Russell and Senator Mark Hatfield.

Frank was Chief of Staff to retired Oregon Senator Mark Hatfield

KEVIN GORMAN

When I turned 25 years old, I was at a crossroads. I was clearly tied to my youth and the good and bad that went with it, yet I was no longer that kid. Instead I was faced with the responsibilities, challenges and opportunities of adulthood. I began taking the steps that would answer the question,"what will I make of myself?"

Our 25-year-old Columbia River Gorge National Scenic Area is at the same crossroads. Its formative years have been impressive: lands preserved, new recreation developed, fierce acrimony subsiding and businesses moving into the Gorge because of its quality of life. The Gorge's beauty and its land protection programs have led to accolades from across the country and around the world.

The Columbia River Gorge National Scenic Area has indeed come far and its accomplishments are worthy of celebration. But not too much celebration. As with any 25-year-old, things are starting to get more complex. Increasing complexity is the cross to bear for preserving a spectacularly beautiful place so close to a major metropolitan area. Development pressures will grow, and in some cases, in ways we can't fathom today. People will love this place, but sometimes love is blind, and our dear Gorge could indeed be loved to death.

By the 50th anniversary, the world will likely know what the Columbia River Gorge National Scenic Area has made of itself. Will it continue to be a model respected and admired around the world? Or will it be a case study for a good idea that simply couldn't overcome the pressures of overdevelopment and commercialization it faces everyday?

The answer of course lies with you. The people who care enough about the Gorge to read this book. Though mere mortals could never create something as majestic and awe-inspiring as the Columbia River Gorge, it is indeed up to us and, as Abraham Lincoln would say, "the better angels of our nature" to preserve this place for those who follow in our paths.

Gorman is executive director of Friends of the Columbia Gorge

Fall and Historic Gorge Highway reflect at Benson State Park TPL

Season's Greetings at Skamania Lodge in Washington

MAUI MEYER

Twenty-five years on and, to my mind, only the first of the really important conversations are being had. As an example of preservation the Scenic Area Act has been a huge success, of that there can be no question. It is remarkable, every time I drive through the Gorge, to see the beauty that was preserved by the legislation.

But that is the point. I'm driving. On a freeway. Six total lanes and two train tracks, and only one of a half dozen corridors coming out of the Pacific West. In that manner, we live in two worlds, one of preservation and the other of exploitation. Have we lived up to that balance? Have we answered, with examples, the question that paradox poses?

The road through the Gorge leads to and from someplace. It brings in goods and services, and it exports resources, and news of the high quality of life enjoyed in the Hood River Valley. It validates, literally, and figuratively, our very existence in the Gorge. To reconcile these items is to understand the fine balance of economy and ecology in our unique context and time. By nature of our "island" in the National Scenic Area, we skew to ecology, but we cannot discount our economy. It feeds us. It shelters us. It allows us to aspire. Ours is a model soon tested, one that has grown in the direction of sustainability, but in a manner pragmatic.

Twenty-five years on and, to my mind, only the first of the really important conversations are being had. How do we choose to live going forward? It's clear now, that we don't – we can't – live to the standards of another homogeneous American place. We are too close to our agriculture, too close to each other, to choose that path.

We pivot then, to face something different. Something … simpler. Technology-enabled, awash in resources, we create a community that honors timber, honors food, honors interdependence, honors our closeness to each other, real and imagined, in times of scarceness and in times of abundance.

Are we brave enough to attempt to live the fusion of our lives and our environment? An example of abundance in the next quarter century? We are. We have. The stage has been set. The table has been set. Twenty-five years on, and only the first of the really important conversations are being had.

Meyer is a Hood River County Commissioner and business owner

Peter Marbach hikes his favorite trail on Dog Mountain in the western Gorge TPL

JACK MILLS

It was a warm sunny Sunday morning in the fall of 1943. Two 13-year-old boys were riding east up the Columbia River Gorge in a small motorboat passing Multnomah Falls. The next morning they would board a train and head to a New England prep-school as their brothers and fathers had done a generation before them.

Not long after my arrival at this school and its foreign surroundings, an English teacher gave my class an assignment, to submit a short paper on the following subject: "If you were to become homesick, about what would that be?" I immediately thought of my sunny warm motorboat cruise up the Columbia River Gorge only a few weeks earlier. I remember that I was asked to read my paper to the class and received an A for it. Thus started my love affair with that beautiful flowing body of water known as the mighty Columbia.

Fast-forward approximately 40 years. Nancy Russell was starting her intense political campaign to create what we now refer to as the Columbia River Gorge National Scenic Area Act. The purpose was to protect the "area" from commercial and residential buildings. My wife Kate and I had known Nancy since high school days. Nancy knew we had moved from Portland to Hood River County, and not wanting to have the non-profit "Friends of the Gorge" look as though it were just a playground for the big city folks in Portland, she asked Kate and me to become members of the "Friends'" first Board of Directors. We accepted, as did several other people who lived across the river from us in Washington. Due to fierce opposition to the project (financial self-interests and property rights issues), the battle became contentious. For me, the next few years were almost a blur. For instance, as a Hood River County Commissioner, I traveled to Washington, D.C. (at my own expense) to offset the testimony of the chairman of our commission (who traveled at county expense). We were both testifying before U.S. Senator Dan Evans of Washington State, and U.S. Senator Mark O. Hatfield of Oregon. Fortunately, both of those Senators were in favor of establishing a Federal National Scenic Area. And as history has shown, the good guys prevailed.

Mills is a former Hood River County Commissioner

ABOUT THE AUTHOR

Janet Cook is an award-winning staff writer for the *Hood River News*, and freelances for other publications. She visited the Columbia River Gorge for the first time in 1985, awed by the landscapes and unaware of the hard work being done to preserve them. She spent several summers in Hood River in the early 1990s and moved there permanently in 1996. She and her husband, Peter Hixson, spend much of their time exploring the Gorge with their two young children. Janet met Peter Marbach 15 years ago when she was assigned to write a story about him for the newspaper. Since then they've become friends and colleagues; this is their third book collaboration.

ABOUT THE PHOTOGRAPHER

Peter Marbach is a renowned landscape photographer with several coffee table books and nationally published work to his credit. The *Columbia River Gorge National Scenic Area* book is his third and most impressive collaboration with his longtime colleague and friend, Janet Cook. His previous books include *Oregon Harvest, Hood River—Land of Plenty, Mount Hood—The Heart of Oregon,* and *Mount Hood—Portrait of a Place*. Peter resides in the heart of the Gorge in Hood River.

In addition to the book titles above, Peter presently does two signature calendars with Beautiful America Publishing Company. They are Beautiful America's *Oregon* and Beautiful America's *Columbia River Gorge*.

www.petermarbach.com

COMING HOME

When I was six, I decided to walk home from school. I was blissfully ignorant that home was ten miles away on lonely back-country roads and that my mother might be worried. The thrill of striking out on my own was short lived when a caring neighbor pulled up and firmly suggested I get into the car. Whatever inspired that impulse remains a mystery, but the innocence and joy of that experience sparked a lifelong reverence to answering the call of the wild.

I owe my embrace of wild places to my mother. As a young boy, she took me for long walks into the woods. I held her hand tightly as the woods felt dark and terrifying but those fears melted away as she pointed out the beauty of the trees and the names of flowers that made me giggle like Jack in the Pulpit and Skunk Cabbage. It was a magical time of learning to be at home in nature. Growing up, the outdoors became the one place I could count on as my anchor having moved seven times by the age of 16. While I longed for a sense of place that comes with putting down roots, I learned to adapt to the frequent moves seeking out wilderness wherever I could find it. While in college, my mother gave me Peter Jenkins book, A Walk Across America. This tale of one man's journey on foot to rediscover America and what he learned about himself struck a defining chord that forever changed my life.

I sought out ways to combine hiking with community service and embarked on a series of fundraising treks along the Appalachian Trail, the length of Great Britain, and the Pacific Crest Trail. It was 1989 when my then fiancée and I descended down the PCT into the heart of the Gorge in Cascade Locks. We were blown away by the beauty of the towering basalt cliffs but equally impressed by the spirit and generosity of a welcoming community. We feasted on burgers and fries and milkshakes at the East Wind Drive In and spent several days at the home of the Reverend Dick Nathe who took pity upon observing our homeless looking appearance.

Serendipity and fate intervened a few years later as an extended car-camping trip from Texas to Oregon brought us back to the Gorge. While visiting a local community health center, my wife was offered a dream job so we pulled up stakes from Maine and landed in Hood River. I figured this would be just another brief chapter in a lifetime of wandering.

With no formal training, I decided to pursue the life of an outdoor photographer. I had developed an eye for beauty, informed by years spent in wilderness observing the magic hours of light at the edges of day. I gradually found work and along the way I began to feel connected to this place. Living in the Columbia River Gorge gave me access to wilderness on any given day. Life was good until unexpected heart surgery shattered my world. This was a different kind of wilderness, but one that felt strangely familiar since time alone in nature takes you on an inner journey. So once again, I turned to the hills for healing. When I could again ascend the wild-flower meadows of Dog Mountain and stand on the summit of Mt Hood at dawn, I knew that I was healed and had finally found my home.

There are places on this planet that have known magnetic force fields that attract creative people. I am convinced that the Gorge is home to a force of nature unlike any other. I am but one of hundreds of painters, sculptors, poets, writers, and artists that have been called to move here. There is a connection to this landscape that goes back to an ancient wilderness, a sense of place that speaks to our own true nature. The towering basalt cliffs and the pathways that lead to their summits stand as cathedrals in a church that is always open, ready to embrace and welcome you home.

Peter Marbach

Beautiful Gorge view from Cape Horn Trail, Washington TPL

Rear cover: Autumn at Beacon Rock Golf Course